A STEP-BY-STEP BOOK ABOUT
HAMSTERS

ANMARIE BARRIE

Photography: Dr. Herbert R. Axelrod, Michael Gilroy, Burkhard Kahl, Courtesy of Penn-Plax Plastics, Brian Seed. Humorous drawings by Andrew Prendimano.

Distributed in the UNITED STATES by T.F.H. Publications, Inc., 211 West Sylvania Avenue, Neptune City, NJ 07753; in CANADA to the Book Trade by Macmillan of Canada (A Division of Canada Publishing Corporation), 164 Commander Boulevard, Agincourt, Ontario M1S 3C7; in ENGLAND by T.F.H. Publications Limited, 4 Kier Park, Ascot, Berkshire SL5 7DS; in AUSTRALIA AND THE SOUTH PACIFIC by T.F.H. (Australia) Pty. Ltd., Box 149, Brookvale 2100 N.S.W., Australia; in NEW ZEALAND by Ross Haines & Son, Ltd., 18 Monmouth Street, Grey Lynn, Auckland 2, New Zealand; in SINGAPORE AND MALAYSIA by MPH Distributors (S) Pte., Ltd., 601 Sims Drive, #03/07/21, Singapore 1438; in the PHILIPPINES by Bio-Research, 5 Lippay Street, San Lorenzo Village, Makati Rizal; in SOUTH AFRICA by Multipet Pty. Ltd., 30 Turners Avenue, Durban 4001. Published by T.F.H. Publications, Inc. Manufactured in the United States of America by T.F.H. Publications, Inc.

Contents

HAMSTERS AS PETS

A good domesticated pet is the type of animal that can withstand the rigors of being bred and raised in captivity, generation after generation, without noticeably declining or deteriorating in health or appearance. In nature, animals do not have to contend with careless handling, filthy housing, poor diets, and the detrimental effects of inbreeding. When the environment is not to their liking, free animals can change their location. They hunt food, defend and hide from predators, and choose their own mate. In captivity, pets can do none of these things. The golden hamster has flourished despite confinement, and breeders have established strong stocks of domesticated hamsters in a variety of color and fur types.

Presently, there are countless millions of hamsters providing entertainment and giving love to their owners. Their gentleness, attractiveness, ease of care, and amusing ways make them especially suitable as pets.

Hamsters are small animals, which means they are inexpensive to feed and maintain. They can live comfortably in relatively small quarters, so a large cash outlay is not needed for housing. Pet shops sell various good, but inexpensive, hamster cages. An idle bird cage or fish aquarium can be used as well.

Hamsters fit snugly into the palm of your hand. They are larger and prettier than mice. It is fun to cuddle them, and you do not have to worry about any odor. In fact, one of the most attractive features of the hamster is a complete lack of odor and a general cleanliness. They are also practically mute,

FACING PAGE:
Hamsters delight in stuffing their pouches with food
to be hidden and then eaten later in private.

Hamsters are great clowns and love to perform acrobatic stunts.

so they cannot utter any annoying noises. Hamsters are an ideal pet in homes or apartments that are too small for other domesticated animals.

In addition, hamsters are naturally tame and gentle, requiring only a short training period to make them friendly pets. Especially docile are grown males and unbred females, although males generally make the best pets.

Hamsters are quite entertaining. They sit up, stand on their hind legs, and climb and grasp whatever is within reach. Grasping can be done with their hind feet as well. They enjoy performing acrobatic stunts. They relish being hand-fed, played with and fondled. You will find their fur soft and pleasing to the touch. And they are rather cute, too. They come in an assortment of colors and textures, including longhaired and shorthaired forms.

Most pets demand daily care and attention, but hamsters can be left alone over a weekend because they hoard food and don't drink much. If you do venture out for an extended trip and don't take your pet, it will be necessary to have a reliable person look in on the hamster every two days. The food and water must be replenished, and the cage cleaned weekly. Of course, a hamster is easily transported to a new location for safekeeping while you are gone, but you may like to take it with you. Hamsters have been known to thoroughly tolerate traveling vacations!

Hamster's hoarding instinct makes them particularly amusing to observe. You will be intrigued as you watch your pet cram food into its cheek pouches and then take it out to hide for another time. The hamster truly delights in taking the food, stuffing its pouches, and scurrying off to a secret corner of the cage, where it can dislodge the contents and leisurely eat the hoarded food at a later date. In fact, a well-stocked food pile is extremely important and comforting to a hamster. A wise owner will not often disturb the hoarded treasure and disrupt his hamster's sense of well-being.

This little fellow enjoying an almond is called a Chocolate Banded Roan.

Hamsters are very inquisitive and love to explore. By not allowing them the run of the house, you will be protecting them from their own mischievous natures.

Hamsters are rugged and easy to breed. In fact, their 16-day gestation period makes them unique in their ability to reproduce. Their life span is about 1000 days, so if you want to be free of hamsters, just stop breeding them. In less than three years their life cycle will have ended. But if you want a family of them, or you want some unusual presents for family and friends, you do not have long to wait for a new batch of young.

Golden hamsters are most obliging in captivity, being such clean, friendly, and inquisitive animals. They want only to explore, to play, to hide, to hoard food, to keep clean with fresh bedding, and to be handled gently. At times, your pet may escape and become lost, but it will be happy to be returned to its cage. Once you understand your hamster's habits, and provide for its needs, training will be easy. Unlike its European relation, the Syrian or golden hamster is usually tame, intelligent and friendly to humans.

Hamsters demand privacy from humans, all other animals, and most other hamsters. They have a strong sense of possession and do not take easily to having their property disturbed. Do not intrude into your hamster's cage unless you

Hamsters are nocturnal creatures and like to sleep most of the day.

would like to have your hand nipped. A sure sign that it is annoyed with you will be that its ears are curled or laid back.

The golden rule for housing hamsters is *one hamster, one cage.* A few young specimens of the same sex may live together in peace if given ample space, plenty of hiding places, and enough food. Males will generally get along better than females, but fights may still occur over territory and food. Even well-tamed hamsters are not easy to keep together in pairs. They will fight to the death if left alone together. Females can

Hamsters, even white ones, are very clean and never need to be bathed, although some like to cavort in a dish of water.

tolerate males only for a short time during mating. If a male is introduced into her cage before she is ready, she could kill him. There are, of course, some exceptions, but avoid trouble by keeping the sexes separate. If you plan to keep several hamsters together in one cage, carefully watch for signs of fighting and part them immediately. Large numbers of hamsters may be kept in large quarters. It's 2 or 3 which, when kept alone, will fight.

Hamsters are nocturnal animals, sleeping during the day and performing over 90% of their activities when their cages are in darkness. If you provide your pet with an exercise wheel, it will probably run from four to eight miles each night on it. If you sleep very lightly, this may be bothersome. Hamsters do not care for sunlight nor any bright light. Nevertheless, you can play with your hamster during the day if you wake it gently and keep it from bright light until it is thoroughly alert.

They are easily alerted and ready to play when their attention is aroused. Breathing heavily or blowing on your hamster will annoy it. Always be thoughtful and patient with your pet and you will get along well.

Baby hamsters will soil the cage anywhere because they are not yet "housebroken". By the time they are about two months old, they will instinctively establish a toilet. Otherwise, grooming hamsters is quite simple. Their teeth and nails wear down as they grow and need no further attention. Hamsters never need a bath; they will groom themselves as long as they are healthy. Even the coat of the longhaired variety infrequently requires an occasional brushing with a dry toothbrush.

Male hamsters do not participate in any family activities. They may destroy the young, or may themselves be killed by the females if they venture too near the babies. All hamsters are very possessive about what is theirs, including their homes, babies, and hoard. Your pet might nip at your hand if you thrust it into the cage, but that same animal will probably be perfectly safe, friendly and tame outside of the cage. There are exceptions, however.

Hamsters are very inexpensive to purchase and feed. They require little maintenance and reproduce rather easily. With proper care, your pet will be free of disease and likely to live out its lifespan of 1000 days.

Hamsters like the dark. In nature they live in deep tunnels.

Select your hamster only from a reputable pet shop. The dealer will be familiar with his sources of supply, so he sells only healthy animals. The employees will be well informed, and the livestock will be of good quality.

SELECTION

A few minutes of observation will probably convince you that owning a hamster would be fun. Be prepared to pay a reasonable price for it, though, because a hamster that costs too little is not really a bargain. Stay away from inferior specimens or laboratory test survivors. Instead, buy hamsters which are sold for breeding stock. Prebreeders will be about the size of the palm of your hand, breeders slightly longer, weighing about three to four ounces. The price of the breeding stock will vary with its quality, but an ethical operator will give you a fair deal.

The hamster should weigh an ounce and a half or more. Its general shape and appearance are very important. The color should be a rich, uniform, golden tan. Even young hamsters should have a chunky build and a short neck. The head should be well-rounded, not tapered and rat-like. The ears should be large and set well apart. Dark, prominent eyes should be bold and bright, expressing inquisitiveness and curiosity. Other signs of good health are soft, silky fur with a bit of sheen, a plump body, and a general feeling of solidity. No protrusions should be felt, and no long white guard hairs should be seen along the hamster's sides. The nose should be slightly damp, but not wet, and the hamster should be eating well.

The animal should be alert and responsive to stimuli, but not jittery or nervous when you approach. In fact, it should be calm and tame enough for you to pick it up. If close inspection re-

FACING PAGE:
Like a squirrel, this Cream Angora hamster is very busy filling its cheek pouches with goodies to eat later.

veals lumps, bumps, discoloration, loose hair, wet bottom or tail, stuffed or running nose, watery eyes, blood anywhere on the body or a nasty disposition, then do not buy that hamster. An animal with pimples on its ears, nose, feet or belly also needs to be passed over. The pimples may be the beginning of mange and mean endless work for you. No cure is guaranteed and it is slightly contagious. Accept only a perfectly healthy pet. Occasionally hamsters with nicked ears are sold as breeders. This hole may be a breeder's mark for identifying members of a certain herd, or it may be the result of a bite from a cage-mate. It is not a disease, and can be safely ignored unless you plan to exhibit your pet competitively.

Hamsters are available in shorthaired and longhaired varieties. (The latter tends to cost a bit more). They are also bred in a variety of colors. The more common are the albino, which is white with pink eyes; the pied, harlequin or panda, which are

Hamsters can use their little hands to hold their food, make their beds, climb, and clean themselves.

The hamster has bold, bright, and curious eyes, but its eyesight is not particularly good.

all spotted brown or beige on white with dark eyes; and a cream, beige or fawn variety with brown or ruby eyes.

Pink-eyed hamsters are likely to have poorer vision than dark-eyed types. In fact, some pink-eyed hamsters are blind or nearly blind. Of all hamsters, remember that the most hardy is the common golden variety.

The best time to purchase your hamster is shortly after it has been weaned from its mother—around five weeks old. If you buy one under 30 days old, its body will be too immature for it to cope with new surroundings. The baby is too young to move, too young to play with and too young to have good control of its responses and locomotion. Young hamsters have even poorer vision than adults, so it is very difficult for them to see things and to judge distance. A baby might scurry right over the edge of a table and onto the floor. This could be hazardous, because unlike cats and mice, hamsters do not naturally flip about in the air and land lightly on their feet.

A mature hamster, say a year old, has already lived a good part of its life. Since the average lifespan is only 1000 days, from the standpoint of cost an older hamster is a poor investment.

Hamsters replace their fur about every three months. In a young specimen, the inside ear is covered with white hairs. As the animal ages, there is a tendency for less hair to appear on

the ears, until all the hair gradually disappears. Do not select a hamster with naked, shiny ears indicating it is past its prime.

Since both males and females make good pets, your hamster can be of either sex. A pair could supply hundreds of good pets. But do not buy a pair unless you know in advance what to do with the offspring. Pet shops can probably obtain their necessary supply of stock from commercial breeders. And never choose your hamster from a cage containing both sexes or you may unexpectedly find yourself with an unwanted family from a much too young female.

Males do seem to be a bit friendlier and more even-tempered than females. Females tend to be slightly larger and heavier, but the male longhair seems to have the slightly longer coat.

When the young are about eight days old and still hairless, two rows of dark spots can be seen on a female's belly—the teats. From the time the fur appears until the young are 18 days old, sexing is particularly difficult. As the animals mature, it becomes easier.

Adult males have one or two black dots over each hip under the fur. These spots are about as large as a hamster's eye and about two to three times the thickness of the skin. They are dimorphic pigment spots, similar to beauty marks in humans. Other large lumps, boils, abscesses and pimples are another matter.

The female hamster has three external orifices, all lying close together in a straight line. The most anterior is the small, raised urinary papilla. A slight groove leads from this to the vagina to the rear of it. Most posterior is the anus. In fully mature animals, the vagina and anus are surrounded by darker pigment.

The male hamster has two external openings, the penis and the anus. The penis is raised and prominent, located in front of the anus. By weaning time, the distance between the two is clearly seen, with a seam or line running between them. Usually the males show a swelling that comes to a tapered fullness near the tail. Females are blunt. However, the shape of the rear is not always a true guide, for a male non-breeder is often as blunt as a female. An experienced operator can easily sex a hamster by resting its body in a supine position in the palm of his hand.

A respectable breeder or dealer will not sell a hamster of infe-

rior quality because he has a reputation to protect. However, you may like to take your new pet to a vet before bringing it home. Make an arrangement with the seller for a refund or exchange if the vet declares your hamster is unfit.

The hamster's senses of hearing and smell are very good. If your fingers smell like food, don't try to pick up your hamster. He might accidentally nip you.

TAMING

Allow your hamster to get used to you and its new surroundings before you pick it up—hamsters bite. If you tease a caged hamster, handle it badly, or poke your fingers into its cage, it may nip you. Usually the bite is so quick and small that the shock hurts more than the wound. The bites are not poisonous, but wash the area well. As your pet becomes accustomed to you, it may be perfectly all right to reach into the cage, but do not do it for the first few days.

Hamsters like human company and look forward to having a fuss made over them. Just tap gently on the cage and call your pet by name. On no account should you lift it out of its bed while it is still asleep. This only makes a hamster cross and you will likely have your fingers bitten. Do not blow or breathe heavily on the hamster either, to awaken it. A sure sign that your pet is annoyed with you will be that its ears are curled or laid back. This often happens when you wake or disturb it. Just be patient. The ears will soon straighten and it will no longer be annoyed.

Upon wakening, your hamster will run to the toilet area and then to the front of the cage to see who is outside. Gently stroke it to let it adjust to the smell of a human hand. (Be sure there is no odor of food on your hands or the hamster may try to hoard your finger in its pouch taking it for a piece of food.)

Do not attempt to pick up your pet at this time. Just keep stroking it for a few minutes, then offer a treat. Soon the hamster will accept food from your hands.

Let your hamster walk out of the cage onto the wire

FACING PAGE:
Hamsters love to climb and play. They're fun to
watch, but keep them safe.

door or onto a table. Then allow it to return to the inside of the cage where you have placed a little treat. The hamster gradually gains confidence in you. It knows no harm is intended.

Let the hamster climb onto your hand. Once it has become accustomed to being touched and handled, eventually close your hand around its body. Lift the hamster gently by cradling its body in your hands. Do not grasp it by the tail, leg, around the neck, or by the loose skin on the neck. Always support the full weight of its body in your hand.

A hamster well adjusted to handling will not struggle, but will stay settled comfortably on the hand, allowing you to stroke it gently. The hamster must learn that your hands don't mean harm, for if frightened it may leap from your fingers, fall, and injure itself.

Young hamsters should be handled daily from the time they are self-sufficient until they are about three months old. They are naturally tame, and to keep them this way they must be handled constantly. Up to this time, youngsters are far too

Hamsters like human company and look forward to having a fuss made over them.

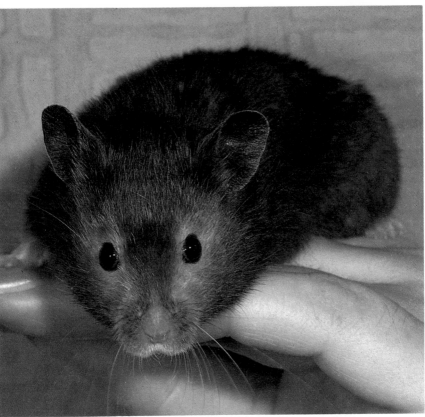

Handled correctly from the start, your pet will soon become so tame it will want to be petted and held all the time.

active to be taught any tricks, but they can become accustomed to human contacts.

Hamsters cannot really learn tricks, nor can they react to a human voice. The secret of training a hamster to perform lies in reinforcing their habitual, spontaneous reaction as a part of their normal life. Using whistled sounds as commands, a continual training routine, and food rewards may enable the hamster to establish a habit. A great deal of time and patience is required on your part.

HOUSING

Housing for hamsters comes in a variety of designs—from simple homes for a single pet to elaborate arrangements used by commercial breeders. Cages purchased from your local petshop are convenient to use, economical, and readily available. You can even find hamster kits which include a cage, feed, cedar chips, a water bottle and just about anything else you may require. As a rule, buy, don't build. Anything you make can probably be bought for less, and it will likely be better. A cage manufacturer has worked out bugs you never even thought of.

For a small-scale home hobbyist, consider a large metal birdcage, or a cage especially for small rodents. A ten gallon all glass aquarium is ideal since most petshops sell "leakers" very inexpensively, and the hamster does not care if the tank leaks water or not. If an aquarium is used, buy a fitted screen top or ⅜ wire mesh cover that locks in place, allowing plenty of ventilation yet preventing a hamster from knocking the top off and escaping.

Choose a cage as large as possible, at least one square foot. Hamsters pile up bedding material at one location and use another site free of covering material to urinate and defecate, thus making it easy for you to clean the cage. The bedding will require changing less often than if the animal had no special place to deposit waste. As far as depth is concerned, six inches is minimum because hamsters spend a lot of time in an upright position eating, drinking, and exploring.

A hamster's home needs to be easily cleaned. Therefore, avoid cages made of wood. Although they may be cheaper than other cages, they are not practical. The wood will soak up urine and will remain damp. Urine-soaked wood takes on a pu-

FACING PAGE:
Selective breeding has resulted in many color types,
but the golden hamster is still the most popular.

trid odor and becomes a breeding ground for disease-causing germs. Cages made of plastic, glass, or stainless steel are all highly recommended. A plastic or metal cage is easily cleaned, light enough to be transported; they require very little maintenance to keep them in good condition.

Furthermore, like all rodents, hamsters like to gnaw, and it would not take long for your pet to chew through a wooden cage bottom. If the wood is splintery and sharp, it can hurt the hamster's mouth or cheek pouches. Metal cages are

For ease of care and cleanliness, a factory-made hamster cage is the best. Cages are available from your pet shop in many styles and sizes.

especially resistant to damage caused by gnawing, and many plastic cages can also withstand a hamster's constant gnawing.

There is really no need for interior food containers or to scatter a hamster's food on the cage floor. A food hopper or feeding chute opening into the cage simplifies feeding and prevents a hamster from piling bedding material over the food or from soaking it with urine when the food is placed loosely in

Housing

Make sure the cage you choose is secure so that your hamster can't escape or predators get in.

the cage. An interior water dish is to be avoided because your hamster will deliberately fill it with litter and wastes. Hamsters are desert animals, and though they can drink water from a dish, standing water is foreign to them. Access to water is best handled with an inexpensive, conventional water bottle that cannot be spilled or dirtied. This consists of a bottle containing a cork or rubber stopper with a metal, glass, or plastic drinking tube inserted into it. The bottle is hung upside down from the side or top of the cage by means of a clip. It should be positioned so water can be lapped from the tube while the animal is in a standing position. The end of the tube will probably be about five or six inches from the bottom of the cage. A bottle with a stainless steel drinking tube is preferred because a hamster's constant gnawing can damage a plastic tube and crack a glass one.

Any cover should have a simple but strong latch that is easy to lock, but not easy for your pet to unlock. Hamsters are great escape artists. This cover should also provide good ventilation. A coarsely screened cover will be of interest to a hamster for exercise. Your pet will climb about upside down for many hours. The cover will also receive its share of gnawing, so be sure it is sufficiently strong.

A well-stocked petshop will have various toys to provide your pet with amusement. Do not use children's toys because hamsters chew on the plastic and it might be toxic if they swallow some. An exercise wheel is a great accessory if there is room for it in the cage and you do not mind the squeaking of the bearings. Your pet may run from four to eight miles each night. The exercise is necessary to prevent paralysis.

A very useful accessory item is a plastic, glass, metal or cardboard scoop a bit larger than your hamster. There are times when it is more convenient to move hamsters in a container such as retrieval before your pet hamster is tame, when cleaning the cage of a mother and her young, or while transferring a female to the cage of a male for breeding. The scoop protects you from being bitten, and it prevents the female from picking up the scent of your hand before she is introduced to the male for breeding. A large mouthed glass jar, a round pound-sized rolled oats box, a plastic bottle with the bottom removed, and other kitchen utensils are all excellent for transportation. Place a handful of food in the receptacle and scoop up the animal. While it is busy stuffing its pouches, the hamster can be moved anywhere.

Place plenty of litter or bedding in the cage which your hamster can move around. A one to two inch layer of commercial bedding is best. The bedding material can be nearly anything which is not poisonous, overly aromatic, sharp or entangling. Torn paper towels, wood chips, wood shavings, mowed hay, and chopped hay have all been used successfully. Ground corn cobs, cane, peanut shells, or anything else clean and absorbent is adequate. Cotton fibers tend to get caught in the hamster's feet, and sawdust is not very satisfactory as it can be easily thrown out of the cage and tends to pack down rather tightly when wet. Urine-soaked sawdust quickly becomes foul, and like a wooden cage bottom becomes a breeding ground for bacteria. A longhaired hamster may get some wood shavings tangled in its hair, but with a dry toothbrush you can smooth the tangles before they become troublesome. Wool or flannel scraps are appreciated by a nesting female since they make warm, soft linings. Tissue paper, though, may stick to the hairless young.

Housing

Many people use cedar chips for the hamster's bedding. Your hamster will re-decorate its cage to its own liking and will be quite miffed if you interfere.

Spread lots of bedding over the bottom of the cage which the hamster can move around to suit its needs; don't pile it up in one corner of the cage. Your hamster will hide food in certain areas, build its nest elsewhere, and sweep clean the spot where it leaves waste. This rearrangement creates another cage consideration. Some metal cages are constructed with a wire top and sides, with only a two-inch closed barrier along the bottom edges of the sides. As the hamsters move the material around, quite a bit of the bedding is scattered about the outside of the cage. Therefore, if a metal cage is used, it should have a solid back and sides, with a barrier across the front of at least three to four inches in height. Some cages come with a removable clear plastic barrier along the cage front. This allows you to see the hamster at all times and also keeps the litter in the cage.

Hamsters themselves have no external parasites, and with a little help from you, a weaned hamster will develop good toilet habits. The urine is the problem, since the feces tend to dry out quickly and dry droppings are virtually odorless. Clean the cage often enough to keep the urine spot localized. If the

entire cage is dirty and damp, your pet has no reason to choose a particular place to wet. Each day, as the waste evaporates, scrape up the remainder and then blot up the last traces with a small wad of bedding which should then be thrown away. Hamsters tend to pile up bedding material at one site and use another location having a bare bottom for waste, making it easy for you to mop the wetness. This also means that the bedding will have to be changed less often than it would if the

This little guy looks lonely, but hamsters actually prefer to be alone in their cages.

hamster did not single out a location to deposit waste. A large enough cage allows a hamster to set up these separate locations.

The floor litter needs to be removed entirely at weekly intervals and replaced with fresh litter. If you clean the cage too frequently, you may unsettle the hamster by disturbing its hoard often. A pancake turner makes a good tool with which to scoop and scrape the floor.

Of course, if you have a cage with a wire bottom through which droppings can fall, your work is simplified, but a hard mass of solidifed urine will still form. This must be broken off every few weeks and the floor scrubbed with a wire brush.

Thorough cage cleaning is an essential part of your regular routine. Every few weeks wash the cage with hot, soapy water and a stiff brush. A mild disinfectant can be added, but do not use insect sprays or dusts since some may be lethal to your pet. By frequently providing fresh bedding, insects and their eggs will be entirely eliminated or kept well under control without the use of insecticides.

A hamster will play with a toy like this for hours. It's good for them to be able to exercise and fun for you to watch.

It is important to clean the cage of a female while she is being mated. At this time she is too busy to be bothered by your cleaning. Afterwards, she will establish a nursery in anticipation of her litter. Except for the solid corner, her cage should not be thoroughly cleaned until the cubs' eyes are open. The rest of the cage contents should be left alone. Since this time lapse is about four weeks, a good idea is to provide plenty of extra bedding material during this period.

If you expect to introduce additional hamsters to your stock, a cage should be kept empty and apart—preferably in another room—as quarantine for new or sick animals. Cages of sick hamsters require thorough washing and disinfecting before they are used again. The cage should have a private area for

Hamsters spend much of their time looking for escape routes, not necessarily because anything's wrong—that's just what hamsters do.

Housing

Water bottles like this one supply your pet with fresh, clean water all the time.

sleeping and hoarding, and enough space for a toilet area. You must provide water, adequate ventilation, and dry, warm cage litter. Hamsters ask for very little, just a simple diet and a draft-free cage. They are very fussy about their beds particularly, and will spend a lot of time making a nest, only to move it if they feel a draft. Do not place the cage in direct sunlight or any other bright, glaring light. Keeping it in an area with an average temperature of 68°F is preferred.

Hamsters will thrive satisfactorily in temperatures ranging from 50° to 80°F, but they can adjust to any climate and humidity. They can be safely outdoors as long as they are protected from the cold. When the air is moist and cold, your hamster may hibernate, so provide a draft-free sleeping area when it is kept outdoors. While adult hamsters can endure even freezing temperatures, the naked young should be raised in a sheltered place. An overhanging roof will give protection from the elements, and ample nestling material is needed during very cold weather.

Discontented hamsters are typically those that are crowded, deprived of privacy, not permitted to hoard, or abused by owners or cagements. However, even a happy hamster will continually try to escape because of its natural curiosity.

ESCAPES

Any hamster spends much of its time gnawing, scratching, digging and attempting to escape. Your pet can maneuver through an opening as large as its head. Since they are such small animals, an adult can crawl through spaces the size of a quarter, and a baby through openings less than one-half inch. It is likely that your hamster will find its way out at least once, but to lessen the possibility, make sure the cage is as strong and as tight as possible. Periodically check the entire cage for the effects of gnawing, especially any areas made of wood. Replace or reinforce any worn spots. All cage openings require an outside latch.

An escaped hamster may pick up parasites, ticks, fleas, or disease and introduce them to cagemates when it is cap-

Your pet shop will have a good supply of hamster accessories like this rock formation; just don't overcrowd the cage.

tured and returned to the cage. Another possibility is the loss of your pet to a predatory animal, like a dog, cat, or rat. A hamster cannot run fast enough to escape them.

The chances of finding an escaped hamster are not in your favor. Hamsters are fond of pipes, tubes, conduits, tunnels, and similar long, dark spaces. They are well hidden in closets, televisions, pianos, and under furniture. But though you may not find your pet by searching, it can be captured easily enough. All you need is a carrot, a deep pail or wastebasket with smooth sides, and a few bricks or blocks of wood. Another hamster (preferably a female if the escapee is a male) will also help, as will some bedding taken from your hamster's cage.

As soon as you realize your hamster is missing, clear the area of any and all predatory animals. Cover all toilets and drains, and empty the bathtubs and sinks. Before going to bed, place the pail on the floor. Arrange the bricks to form an outside stairway leading up to the rim of the pail. Rub the carrot up the "steps" and then leave it in the bottom of the pail. Surround the carrot with some of the cage litter. If you have another hamster, place it on the floor (in its cage) alongside the pail. In the morning, your hamster will be in the pail with the shavings, munching on the carrot!

Commercial traps also work. Most are tunnel-shaped with one or two doors at the ends and a treadle in the center. Bait the treadle with something sticky, like peanut butter or honey, and press some grain into it.

Your hamster will run four to eight miles a day in an exercise wheel like this. Without exercise your pet would soon become bored and listless.

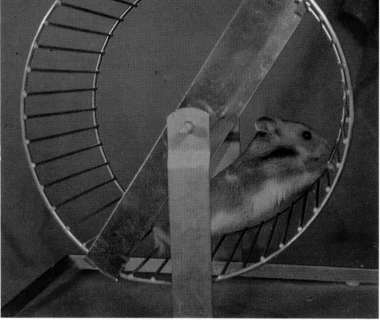

Proper feeding of hamsters is crucial for the maintenance of healthy animals and the production of sound offspring. It is not difficult to supply the right feed or inducing your pet to eat it. Your only responsibility is to offer a variety of well-balanced rations.

FEEDING

Commercial pet food suppliers emphasize proteins in the diet, because they are the main structural components of nearly all living tissue. But feeding hamsters a diet high in protein does not absolutely ensure that they will have all the correct amino acids needed for protein synthesis; thus a seemingly well-fed hamster can suffer from malnutrition. This can be avoided by offering your pet a multitude of proteinaceous foods rather than just one kind of high-protein food. So variety is the key to proper nutrition, but not only variety in the kinds of protein given, but of all the other nutrients as well: the fats, the carbohydrates, the minerals, the vitamins and the fiber. A well-balanced diet produced by a great variety of foods ensures that all of the hamster's physiological functions will be carried out correctly.

The easiest way to get variety in the food supply is to use a packaged mixture designed for hamsters. Used as the mainstay of the hamster diet, these mixes seem to be as complete in their nutrient variety as any single prepared food mix can be, scientifically designed to furnish all the vital substances except water. Some hobbyists never feed their pet anything else but these mixtures, and nothing is wrong with this if you only want your hamster to survive. Unsupplemented by other foods and vitamins, your hamster will grow to almost full size and may or may not breed. However, if you provide treats of

FACING PAGE:
Treats round out your pet's diet and help you tame your hamster easily.

fresh vegetables, fruits, grains, nuts, seeds, and vitamin supplements, your pet will flourish—reaching full size, having brighter colors, displaying more alert behavior, and producing larger and healthier litters.

Fresh fruits and vegetables should not be overlooked, for they are an excellent source of vitamins, minerals, proteins, carbohydrates and roughage or fiber in the form of cellulose. Roughage is a carrier for food material passing through the digestive system. Inadequate roughage means severe digestive disorders. All soft foods should be fed carefully, because green vegetables and fruits do not lend themselves to pouch-packing. The soft, quick-spoiling foods are difficult to remove from the pouch and remain stuck there, causing various health problems. Since they are often eaten on the spot, they make an excellent treat for hand feeding during taming and training.

Nearly any vegetation fit for human consumption is suitable for your pet; potatoes, water chestnuts, watermelon rinds, banana peels, grapes and any vegetable trimmings discarded by your grocer. A convenient and inexpensive method of obtaining green foods for your hamster is to pick up these discarded greens regularly from the grocer, who will probably be glad to give them to you. Thus you have a year 'round source of fresh food. (Do not feed your pet any discarded foods that are not fresh enough for you yourself to eat.)

Even wild plants suit your hamster's dietary needs. Grass, dandelions, clover and chickweed are commonly available and readily eaten. Many people, though, are not good at identifying wild plants and might choose one that can sicken or kill a hamster. Therefore, select only vegetation which is easily identifiable as safe. In addition, keep away from henbane, oak leaves, buttercups, laurel leaves and hemlock. Avoid areas where other domestic animals deposit their wastes, and locations in which herbicides, fungicides and insecticides have been used recently. Before giving any foods to your pet, be sure they are clean and fresh. Remove any dirt and contaminants.

Any of the individual ingredients found in commercial mixtures can be fed alone as a dietary supplement or as a treat. For example, proteins such as barley, wheat, soybeans, wheat germ and whole or cracked corn can be purchased and fed to

your pet. Do not offer oats because the sharp ends tend to scratch the pouch and cause abscesses.

Hamsters are particularly fond of sunflower seeds, which are especially useful for conditioning lactating females, as they seem to enhance milk production. Be sure, however, that once the pups are weaned extra feedings of sunflower seeds are withdrawn from the female's diet. All nuts are rich in fats and carbohydrates; feeding them in excess is fattening. Both sunflower seeds and peanuts serve another purpose for

Luckily, hamsters know what is good (and not good) for them to eat. The black dorsal stripe identifies it as a dwarf hamster.

hamsters besides nutrition. The animals chew the shells into fine fibers to be piled up and used for bedding material.

Pre-packaged mixtures of seeds, especially rape and millet, sold as bird food are also excellent dietary supplements for adult hamsters. Served alone, they make a good first solid food for babies.

Hamsters enjoy nibbling on dry plant stalks like alfalfa, which is packaged and sold as rabbit food. This also makes a suitable nesting material.

Most owners feed their pets some sort of pelletized dried vegetable material designed for small mammals. These commercially prepared foods are nutritionally adequate, inexpensive, convenient, and readily available in pet stores. The pellets, which must be fresh, need to be stored in air tight, moisture-proof containers in a cool, dry place. Cleaned out coffee

cans or a trash can with a tight fitting lids make for good storage. Often spoiled food cannot be detected until it is fed to your hamster, so any food that is suspect should be discarded and the container sterilized before using it again. Fortunately, most unsafe or unwholesome foods will be rejected by your pet.

Although much of the needed water is obtained from soft foods, a supply of fresh, clean water at all times is an absolute must. A separate supply of milk is a valuable addition to any hamster's diet, particularly bred females, nursing females, and newborns. In the babies, it promotes the development of healthy bone structure, thus preventing loss of calcium and ensuring continued productivity in the matron. A newborn will be nursed by its mother until its eyes open and the fur grows. At this time, whole wheat bread soaked in milk should be supplied. This is a great food for the baby and a fine supplement for its mother. Evaporated, condensed, or pasteurized milk can all be given, but never offer raw milk. Check the milk supply often, as milk tends to sour quickly. Slightly older hamsters, as well as breeding females, benefit from a treat of mashed hard-boiled eggs.

Garlic and onions are totally unsuitable, and citrus fruits are controversial. You might try feeding a bit to your hamster and see how it reacts. Introduce any new food in small quantities and only one new food at a time.

The availability of cooked and raw meats is another topic of controversy. Some authorities maintain that meat should not be fed at any time, presuming that it encourages cannibalism of young by their mothers. Others heartily disagree. If you choose to feed your hamster meat, do so on a trial basis. If the results seem to be satisfactory, continue the feedings. Your pet will at least get some enjoyment from boiled beef bones, while at the same time deriving some value from the minerals in the bone. Small, hard dog biscuits or kibble are high in calcium and phosphorus, thereby promoting strong bones, teeth and claws. Dry pellets, bones, and biscuits also give hamsters plenty of gnawing exercise, since they are good tooth-grinding mediums. Petshops also sell special chew treats for hamsters that keep their teeth in condition.

Vitamin and mineral supplements are recommended for your pet, especially if you are planning to breed it. Wheat germ oil, cod liver oil, and other fish oils make for good vitamin supplements. These liquid supplements may be offered in the drinking water, sprinkled on food, or given through an eye dropper. Ripe whole wheat as it comes from the stalk and raw peanuts are prime sources of Vitamin E.

Hamsters are slow eaters and constant nibblers. They are designed and equipped to consume hard materials, like nuts and seeds, that are slowly chewed and slowly digested. Just because your hamster accepts what you offer and stuffs it into its pouches doesn't mean that it plans to eat or use the material at that time. Your pet just wants to carry it off for later use. Whether you feed a hamster each day at a specific time, or simply replenish the stock when it is low, it is the hamster who decides when and what to eat. Hamsters eat only for their immediate needs, so don't be afraid of offering too much food. Since they do not overeat, you cannot overfeed them. What they don't eat will just be hidden away.

Even though hamsters are desert animals, they need a steady supply of fresh water.

Without opening its eyes, your pet may reach for a bite during the day, but being night creatures, they will usually wait for their main meal in the evening. Your hamster may even eat while it still looks asleep, with partially or fully closed eyes. Under natural conditions, hamsters eat underground, so eyesight is not important for managing food.

Due to the hoarding instinct, you must avoid feeding excess food which spoils or smells as it ages. The method of presenting is an important factor in the health of your hamster. Food can be sprinkled directly into the cage, placed in a small dish on the cage bottom, or put in a food hopper. However, the simple scattering of food into the cage is not recommended because the food will get piled under bedding material and mixed with wastes. A hamster is not likely to eat this contaminated food, but its spoilage is foul smelling and provides a breeding ground for germs. The cage will have to be cleaned more often than with other feeding methods.

Placing food in a dish or bowl minimizes the scattering of food, although some will still get mixed with bedding mate-

Hamsters will eat many things that people eat, but not everything we eat is good for them.

rial and wastes. The feeding dish should be heavy enough so that your hamster cannot push it around or easily topple it over.

Special feeders and hoppers are commercially available. The food is placed into the container, which is typically built into the lid or side of the cage. The hamster can remove the amount of food desired through a small opening at the bottom of the hopper.

Your hamster will be delighted to crawl into a pipe or tunnel. Unfortunately, if it escapes, it might get into serious trouble "tunneling."

If your watering system is reliable, you can safely leave your hamster unattended for a few days. Leave enough grain and water (about two tablespoons of water and one tablespoon of food for each day) for nourishment while you are gone. A piece of raw potato or apple will fulfill any need for extra moisture. Hamster cages are easily transported, though, if you would like to take your pet along for the ride!

AILMENTS

Hamsters have no known diseases of their own. They are rugged, hardy creatures that can live their lifetime of 1000 days with minimum trouble. Well-fed hamsters that are kept in a clean environment rarely contract disease, because their resistance is kept at its peak when they are properly maintained. Many diseases can be cured or prevented by using clean bedding and changing it before it becomes an invitation to vermin, and their dietary regimen is simple enough. Your pet should have plenty of hard grains to store, but don't provide any more soft foods than it will eat, not hoard, immediately. Disinfect the cage regularly, and always offer fresh drinking water.

Of course, accidents do happen, but do your best to prevent them. Handle your hamster with care and treat it with thoughtfulness. It is not a great climber, much less an acrobat or a flier. Protect your pet from falls, careless children, and predatory animals. It is far better to avoid mishaps, escapes, and injuries by keeping the cage lock fastened.

Hamsters are subject to the same sort of ailments as man: injuries, nutritional diseases, and infectious diseases. So keep visitors away from hamsters as much as possible. Protect them from yourself when you have a cold or some other infection by exercising scrupulous personal cleanliness. Some breeders advise wearing a gauze mask over your nose and mouth. If your pet does become ill, it may recover with care or recover spontaneously. Isolate the ill hamster from any others, and treat it with simple, intelligent care. Take all possible precautions. Always place a newly purchased animal in isolation for a few days before introducing it to the rest of the group. In the

FACING PAGE:
Given proper care and protected from accidents,
most hamsters will live to the ripe old age of about
1000 days.

42

long run, these tips make hamster keeping and breeding an easy and rewarding pastime.

Most hamsters having a lifespan of 1000 days, will die of old age. It is wise to learn as much as you can about them so that you are aware of the limitations. Should your hamster appear ill, do not hesitate to take it to a qualified veterinarian. Self-doctoring may do more harm than good. If your pet suffers from an incurable disease, let the vet put it to a painless death. This is not meant to be cruel, but rather it will save an infected hamster from a lingering, miserable death. You are also preventing other hamsters from contracting the illness.

SKIN DAMAGE

Small cuts and wounds are usually taken care of by your hamster itself. It will wash and clean the damaged area, which will quickly heal and return to normal.

TEETH

Hamsters' teeth continually grow and they are naturally tinted brown. Keep some chew sticks or pieces of hard dog biscuit in the cage; the gnawing will keep the teeth from becoming overgrown. If your pet should have one of its teeth broken or chipped, it can be trimmed with nail scissors or a nail file.

BALDNESS

Loss of hair in older hamsters is quite normal. When they are from ten to twelve months old, they will begin to lose fur from the rump on upwards. This can be helped by giving your pet a powdered yeast tablet with its food. Loss of hair is also a sign of age. If your hamster loses fur when it is five months old or younger, consult a veterinarian.

SALMONELLOSIS

An intestinal infection which can become epidemic, salmonellosis may be transmitted by wild rodents or dirty drinking water or spoiled foods. A ruffled coat, loss of appetite, weight loss and eventual death can all occur. Treatment and control require destruction of all infected animals. Sterilize the

The name hamster comes from the German *hamstern*, meaning *to hoard*.

cage and all equipment. Start again with fresh bedding, a new food supply, and a healthy hamster.

PNEUMONIA

Pneumona is an inflammation of the lungs indicated by a ruffled coat, loss of appetite, rapid breathing, nasal discharge, coughing, sneezing and catarrh. This typically occurs in poorly nourished colonies of damp and overcrowded animals. The treatment is the same as for salmonellosis.

COLDS

A cold is easily detected by a lack of activity and ears held back against the head. The nose may appear swollen because the fur is ruffled from wiping a nasal discharge. In advanced stages, the hamster gets thin, the fur loses its luster, and sniffling and sneezing can be heard. Disinfect the cage, and all watering and feeding dishes. Provide fresh, dry bedding, and keep the cage draft free. Offer plenty of wholesome foods supplemented with cod-liver oil. As a preventive measure, do not handle your hamster while you have a cold.

WET TAIL

Wet tail is a highly infectious, dreaded disease caused by a tapeworm, which usually proves to be fatal. Often a disease of neglect, damp cages, and spoiled food; malnourished animals are typically indicative. Symptoms include poor general condition, ears laying down, loss of appetite, a jelly-like fluid oozing from the vent, and diarrhea resulting in a very wet tail and dirty hind quarters. A veterinarian may be able to save your pet's life, but death usually occurs in a few days. Disinfect the cage and burn its contents. Discard all food and water containers and clean your hands thoroughly. The control for this disease is obvious.

DIARRHEA

As an isolated disorder, diarrhea is not to be confused with wet tail. It is commonly the result of an overfeeding of vegetables and fruits or contaminated foods. Diarrhea is often indicative of another ailment, such as a stomach upset or a blockage. Discontinue the feeding of fruits and vegetables for a day or two. If the condition persists, consult a veterinarian.

CONSTIPATION

A wet tail can also indicate constipation. In both old and young hamsters, constipation is directly related to the ratio of pellets and water they are eating. In the case of the young, they consume the pellets which swell up in their intestines because they aren't getting enough moisture. Babies suffering from this ailment may be saved by making available milksop and juicy greens. In adults, the same cause is attributable. The hamster seems to waste away because it will not eat dry food if sufficient water is not available. If you have more than one hamster in a cage, be sure that one dominant animal is not taking all the water. Provide plenty of carrots, carrot tops, other leafy vegetables and fruits.

An active hamster is not subject to paralysis, which is caused by inactivity.

MANGE

If your pet shakes its head a lot, scratches its ears, loses its hair, and has a poor general appearance, check for parasitic spiders or insects. The condition is mange, which results in gray, warty scabs on the ears, nose, and genitals. Your veterinarian will probably recommend a medicated bath. Sterilize the cage and all equipment and replace the bedding. Wash your hands well after handling the animal. A high standard of hygiene is the necessary control.

VERMIN AND SKIN DISORDERS

Hamsters spend about 20 percent of their time grooming themselves, so skin parasites are not a common problem. Since a disorder of this type is generally associated with dirty cages, provide clean, dry nesting material so a breeding ground for parasites is not established. In some areas, though, there is a fly, similar to the housefly, that deposits its eggs on nursing mothers or baby hamsters. The maggots then settle in the hamster's skin and steal milk. It grows to half an inch and becomes rather dark, literally digging a hole into your afflicted pet. If you live in such an area, insulate the hamster cage with a fine screen and remove any maggots you find. Fortunately, this is a rare occurrence.

FLEAS AND LICE

These pests can be passed on to your hamster from cats, dogs, rats, and mice. Fleas and lice are not unusual, and if you suspect that your hamster has either of these, sprinkle the nest with flea powder. Check with your pet dealer to make sure that you use a type not harmful to your hamster. Change the bedding before each application so any eggs ready to hatch will be discarded. Be sure to eliminate fleas and lice from all other afflicted household pets.

OVERGROWN NAILS

Clip overgrown nails with nail scissors or a nail clipper, being careful not to trim too close to a blood vessel. Smooth any rough edges with an emery board.

RUNNING EYES

Tears may form in the eyes indicating trouble in the cheek pouches. Soft food may have become stuck back near the shoulder. Flush out the pouch with water of the hamster's body temperature using an eye dropper or syringe. Offer only soft foods that are eaten on the spot. Do not offer excessive amounts that your pet will hoard in its pouches.

LUMPS AND BUMPS

Hard lumps anywhere on the body may be cancerous tumors. Have them checked by a veterinarian.

PARALYSIS

A common ailment which can be avoided is paralysis. Often the result of a lack of exercise, an afflicted hamster will spend most of its time hunched over, often unable to raise its head. Provide a roomy cage, an exercise wheel, or some other activity or recreation to effect a rapid recovery.

Another type of paralysis results from a spinal injury or from a vitamin D deficiency. The first signs are stiffness of the paws, leading to loss of movement in the forepaws, and then slowly to death. Feed your hamster plenty of wheat germ and wheat germ oil. If the disease reaches the advanced stage, it is best to destroy the animal.

Hamsters do not understand words, but can be trained to whistled commands.

INFERTILITY

Sometimes caused by a cold, infertility can also result from a lack of vitamin E in the diet. Hamsters that are constantly annoyed or overweight may experience infertility, too. In some of the new color strains, it is an inherited weakness.

STILLBIRTH

Death at birth is often the result of falls or rough handling of the mother. The injury may previously have gone unnoticed, but at the time of birth, normal delivery is impossible.

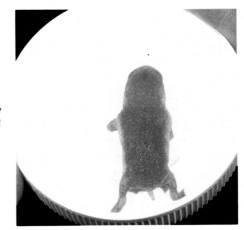

This tiny baby hamster is only one inch long!

BREEDING

Golden Hamsters are fascinating as well as useful animals. One of the great joys of pet-keeping is having your pets reproduce and watching the young grow to maturity. It is small wonder that as the demand for hamsters increases, more and more people become interested in raising them commercially. Their proliferation, gentle temperament, lack of odor, and the ease and economy of caring for them make hamster-raising an inviting occupation. Moreover, many people breed and raise hamsters for exhibition, enjoying the challenge of developing improved strains and of experimenting with new varieties.

Before starting any breeding program, ask yourself a few questions: 1) How many hamsters can you care for? Remember: only one hamster to a cage. 2) Where are you going to keep the breeding stock? The animals must be kept at a steady temperature, not in a place with fluctuations of 10° or more. The area needs to be quiet, free of vermin, and easily kept clean. 3) What will you do with the offspring? Good homes should be previously secured, either with friends, relatives, or a local petshop.

One of the main goals of hamster breeders should be to improve the quality of their stock. Improvement is accomplished by a process of selection favoring desirable qualities and eliminating inferior ones. Start with the best animals available. If possible, your initial pair, or their parents, should possess between them all the qualities you desire. Aim for rich, dense fur; broad, round bodies; bold eyes; erect, uncreased ears; straight backs and good dispositions. Watch stamina and fertility, rejecting any animal which is below standard. With inferior stock, five or six generations may be necessary just to bring the animals up to mediocre quality.

Start with stock of the proper age for breeding purposes. In looking for breeding stock, consider only young specimens. Six-week-old hamsters are ideal because they are not quite old enough to mate, nor are they too old to adapt to new surroundings. Females have been known to breed when they are 28 days old, and they can be safely bred when they are 35 days old; but if you wait until they are eight to ten weeks, your results will be even more satisfactory. A female should be fully grown in order to get good production from her. To properly deliver and nurse all her first litter, a young female should weigh at least 100 grams (3⅓ ounces). A fully mature breeder must weight 150 to 158 grams (5-¼ ounces). Litters from very young and small females are frequently born dead. If the young are too small or too weak, the mother often kills them.

These two hamsters will produce a litter in about 16 days.

Do not wait too long to breed hamsters. The average number of litters born to a female is six, and they should be born and raised while she is still in her prime.

You can tell when a female is in heat, or estrus, by external signs alone. Every fourth or fifth day a white, opaque, mucous plug appears in the opening of the vagina, which is discharged at the end of the cycle. The female is receptive to breeding at the beginning of a cycle, or when there is no discharge. This excretion is the post-estrous discharge, marking the morning of day two of the cycle. The period of sexual receptivity spans the evening of day one into the morning of day two. Fertile matings, though, are limited to the life span of the ova, so the period of fertility is not as long as the period of receptivity. During this time, a female hamster will be much more active, running on a play wheel up to twice the usual revolutions.

Adapt your techniques to the natural habits of the hamster. Since most of their activity takes place in the darkness, sometime in the late evening place an active female in the cage of a male. Do not introduce a male into a female's cage because she is too possessive of her own territory and may hurt the male even if she is in breeding condition. Do not handle her when you are transferring; the lingering human odor may disrupt the pair. Pick her up in some type of scoop, like a jar, can or box.

Within a few minutes, the pair will take note of one another. If there is a little scuffling at first, it will lead to no harm. The female will soon arch her back, raise her tail, and

Observe the differences between these two hamsters. The much smaller one with the black dorsal stripe is the dwarf hamster; the larger is a golden.

stand still if she is receptive. If serious fighting breaks out, stop the hamsters immediately and remove the female. Try again every evening until the female accepts the male. This may take as many as five trials. The actual mating lasts about fifteen to twenty minutes. Afterwards, return the female to her cage. Do not leave her with the male overnight, for she may harm or exhaust him.

The baby hamster's coat will pick up more of the mother's color as it grows.

One helpful hint is to remove all food from the male's cage before installing the female, who may spend much time filling her pouches. She may or may not show the male any interest hence.

During the copulation, clean the female's cage, because for the next 16 days she must be left totally undisturbed (except for refreshing the food and water containers and the usual wiping up of the waste area). Stress during pregnancy could cause developmental birth defects or the female to abort.

The next major cleaning occurs on the 12th day of pregnancy. This gives the female at least four days to rearrange the bedding and build a new nest before the pups are born. She will need enough material to make a nest about six inches in diameter. Provide a large quantity of food to avoid having to open the cage frequently. Do not handle the mother at all, even if she is your pet.

This black-eyed cream mother delivered five ruby-eyed cream babies.

During pregnancy and while nursing, provide a richer than normal diet. High protein foods, like nuts and carrots, and some other source of fat, like sunflower seeds, should be offered. Be sure to provide milk at this time. Soft foods, milk-soaked bread, lettuce, wheat germ and hard-boiled eggs are good for mothers and their babies. The water bottle, or a shallow dish of water, should be well within the reach of the newborn. Care in feeding young hamsters correctly will show up later, so take care to nourish them well, but don't provide too many fattening treats.

These two dwarf hamsters are about 6 months old. The dwarf hamster, from Asia, is a different species from the more common Syrian hamster.

The average number of normal shorthaired hamsters is eight, but can range from two to sixteen. It will take from half an hour up to several hours for a litter to be whelped, depending on its size. The cubs are about an inch long, deep pink, with transparent skin. Weighing from $\frac{1}{14}$ to $\frac{1}{8}$ of an ounce, they are blind, helpless, and completely naked. The young can wiggle about, and during the birth process may become scattered around the nest. Whether they are crying, or even if they appear dead, leave them alone! When the last cub is born, the female will roam through the cage and collect them. If one is dead, it will remain out of the nest; it is then you can remove it. If you touch one of the babies, before the eyes open, (around sixteen days) or you somehow frighten the mother, she may kill one or all of the young, or desert the litter.

If cubs are not produced after 19 days, try the mating technique all over again.

At seven days old, the young are covered with a black guard-coat, except on the belly where their markings will be light. As they mature, the golden fur begins to grow.

Soon the cubs begin to wander about the nest. Both the babies and the mother enjoy scavenging for food, so cut up a mixture of green foods and wheat germ and sprinkle it in the nest. Be sure to provide enough for the entire family, or there may be fights over it.

At 12 days of age, the mother stops cleaning up after the young, and they leave the nest to seek food other than their mother's milk. Now offer carrots and celery tops and grain.

Up to this time, only the soiled corner of the cage has been cleaned. Now that the youngs' eyes are open (about 16 days) the cage can be given a thorough cleaning. Do not separate the mother and the pups, or trouble may occur when they are reunited. The family may act as strangers to one another and serious fighting may break out. As before, do not touch the mother or her babies, but use some type of scoop.

Young raised for commercial purposes can be weaned from 18 to 21 days. Future breeding stock should be left a few days longer. Some breeders wean hamsters when they weigh one ounce.

Well-cared-for hamsters mature quickly. At about the time a hamster is weaned, it is sexually mature, but should not be bred until optimum breeding age and weight are reached. Therefore, hamsters should be sexed and separated early, before their 35th day at the latest. (Hamsters have been known to breed as early as 28 days.) Separation prevents brother-sister matings, and eliminates the possibility of fighting.

If you intend to mate the female again, allow her three or four days to rest. Pregnancy and rearing are draining, and only hamsters in prime condition should be bred.

Be sure to keep records. List the name of every animal, its parents, date of birth, and record its good and bad points. Stillbirths, runts and deformities might account for 2% of the young. If your animals' defect rate is higher, you ought to find out why. Don't breed hamsters that have a poor history of mating.

If a mother kills her babies, it may be because you or some other irritant upset her. If she kills and eats the young, you should suspect a dietary deficiency, probably a lack of calcium and protein. Feed her milk, peas, beans and dog biscuits. If she deserts them, or kills the babies but does not eat them, she may be nervous or insecure. Be sure she is supplied with plenty of bedding and fresh milk, and she gets lots of privacy. First litters from young or undernourished mothers are sometimes killed, but with proper rest and care, the same female will

Mother hamster with her 10-day-old babies.

A litter of tortoise-shell babies.

produce subsequent litters and raise them to maturity without a hitch. These females often mature to become steady breeders of high quality young. In fact, the optimum productivity seems to come from females after their first litter but while they are still in their prime.

HAMSTER SHOWS

In 1945, British fanciers formed their first hamster club. Their aim was to encourage the keeping of Golden Hamsters as pets and to improve them with careful breeding techniques. Shows were organized where qualified judges awarded prizes to the best specimens. As a guide for uniformity, a written description of all desirable features was agreed upon and a certain number of points awarded for each feature. This is known as the "Normal Golden Hamster Standard." If you breed your pet, you should aim for the criteria established in this framework. At that time, no varied shades of the ordinary Golden Hamster existed. More recently, standards have been established for the Golden Agouti and the Golden Fawn hamsters, as well as provisional standards for the Panda and Cream hamsters, but the basic body frame of each type is the same.

NORMAL GOLDEN HAMSTER STANDARD

TYPE

The hamster shall be cobby, well-conditioned in body, with large head, broad skull, and short in face; blunt-nosed, avoiding all ratlike appearance. The head shall be well-set in the body, as short-necked as possible, with the general outline producing a smooth curve from the nose tip over to nape of the neck. The eyes shall be bold and prominent; ears set well apart, large, and of good width, and carried alert when the animal is actively awake.

20 points

COLOR

The top color shall be a rich, deep gold, approaching

FACING PAGE:
This is some handsome hamster!

light chestnut, reaching from nose to tail, free from shading, and of black ticking hairs. Top color carried well down the fur, with a uniform blue-gray under-color at the base of the hairs.

40 points

SIZE

The animal shall be as large as possible, due allowance being made for sex in the mixed classes.

15 points

CHEEK-FLASH AND CRESCENTS

The black cheek-flash shall be clear and deeply pigmented, tapering to a point ending behind the base of each ear; bordered by the rear white crescent, which shall also be clearly defined and as true white as possible. The front white crescent shall be in the form of a short curve up the face.

10 points

CHEST BAND

The chest band shall be unbroken, well furred, and golden brown in color.

5 points

BELLY FUR

The belly fur shall be as nearly white as possible, and of good density.

5 points

CONDITION

The fur shall be soft, short, dense, and glossy; the animal well-fleshed and sturdy.

5 points

PENALTIES FOR ALL STANDARDS
1. Disease or complete intractibility—**Total Disqualification**
2. Wounds, scars, or damaged ears—**Minus 10 points**
3. Dirty staging—**Minus 10 points**
4. White hairs on top-coat, face, etc.—**Minus 5 points**

Sections of the standard may need a little translating. For instance, "cobby" requires the general build of the hamster to be sturdy and thick set. The body length should not be more than 1 2/3 times the width across the hips. The head needs to be large in proportion to the rest of the body, and as wide between the centers of the ears as from the nose to the top of the skull.

A cinnamon-banded, ruby-eyed hamster.

Head shape is also important. The curve of the head from nose tip to neck should be smooth. The face should be short and blunt, ears and nose forming an equilateral triangle. The length of the head should not exceed the distance between the ears. The ideal hamster should not be ratlike in appearance. And the larger the hamster the better, as long as the other features are not lost. But size does not refer to fat. A large skeleton should be covered with firm flesh. Squeeze your hamster gently. Bone and meat will hold firm—fat will give.

HAMSTER SHOWS

1) There are National Hamster Council Shows that are run by an affiliated club for the benefit of the N.H.C.

2) Open shows are shows arranged by mutual agreement between secretaries of clubs affiliated with the N.H.C.

3) Club shows are run primarily for the members of the club holding the show.

4) Handstock shows are those to which all exhibits are brought by the exhibitors, as the title implies. Railstock is not accepted.

5) Sweepstakes shows are those at which the prize monies paid are percentages of the total entry fees for each class.

The following books by T.F.H. Publications are available at pet shops everywhere.

YOUR FIRST HAMSTER—Art by E. Videla
TFH ST-004

Your First Hamster joins this delightful series of basic pet care instruction manuals that lead readers, young and old, through full-color story panels (there are full-color photographs in Your First Hamster, too) depicting in words and pictures the practical first steps to successful hamster to ownership. The large-format 8½ x 11" book is fun to read and enjoy. It makes a great gift, and it's the perfect beginning book for a new hamster owner.

SUGGESTED READING

TEDDY BEAR HAMSTERS—By Mervin F. Roberts
TFH PS-710

Contents: Hamster Facts, Classification And Useful Tables. Hamster Features. You And Your Pet. Choosing A Pet Hamster. Caging. Feeding. Children And Hamsters. Grooming And Bathing. Breeding. Raising Young Hamsters. Genetics. Genetics Glossary. Diseases.

Audience: For breeders and pet keepers a special emphasis on the man-made long-haired hamster variety. The genetics section is entirely new and provides answers and information not otherwise readily available. Grades 8-12.
Hard cover, 5½ x 8", 96 pages
46 black and white photos, 37 color photos

BREEDING HAMSTERS—By Marshall Ostrow
KW-134

This highly detailed book provides all of the information that a first-time hamster breeder is looking for. It includes very practical recommendations about choosing breeding stock, caring for the young, nutritional schedules for breeding hamsters, and a

full section devoted to selective breeding practices.
Hard cover, 96 pages, 5½ x 8"
Contains over 40 full-color photos, many black and white photos.

HAMSTERS—By Percy Parslow
KW-015
Beautifully detailed and explicit, this excellent book furnishes all of the basic information required by anyone starting out with hamsters. It covers everything—choosing your pet, feeding, housing, sexing, breeding, color breeding, purchasing stock, hamster shows and hamster exhibiting, diseases and ailments—highlighted with beautiful full-color photos.
Hard cover, 5½ x 8", 96 pages
Contains almost 50 full-color photos, 47 black and and white photos.

THE T.F.H. BOOK OF HAMSTERS—By Mervin F. Roberts
Contents: Hamsters in General. How to Choose a Hamster. Housing. Feeding. Hamster Diseases. Breeding. Standard Freatures. RAising Young Hamsters. Hints from a Professional. Hamsters in Research.
Audience: Covering every aspect of selecting, housing, breeding and feeding hamsters, this informative volume provides detailed advice for those owning this increasingly popular household pet and is especially valuable for beginners. Disease control and record-keeping are covered in special sections.
Hard cover, 8½ x 11", 80 pages; 89 full-color photos

Index